History Insights

STUARTS

CONTENTS

Educational consultant: John Cook

Donna Bailey

Headway · Hodder & Stoughton

WHO WERE THE STUARTS?

Elizabeth I never married and died childless in 1603, bringing an end to the House of Tudor.

For the rest of the century the kings and queens of England came from the House of Stuart, except for a period between 1649 and 1660. During this time the country was ruled by Parliament and Oliver Cromwell.

▼ James I 1603-1625

James I's mother, Mary Queen of Scots, was the great granddaughter of the Tudor king Henry VII. James became King James VI of Scotland in 1567, while still a baby. In 1603, James became king of England as well as Scotland. He was warmly welcomed by many people in the towns and villages through which he passed on his way to London. However, he was so extravagant that he was often short of money, and soon became unpopular with both Parliament and the people. Some called him 'The wisest fool in Christendom', meaning that although he was clever, he had no common sense.

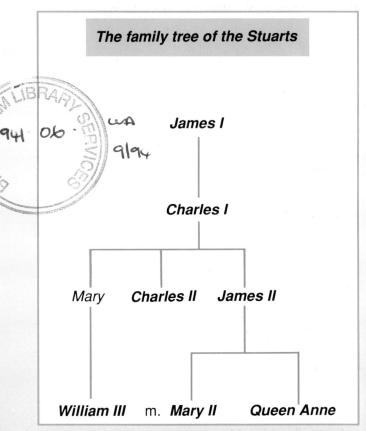

The family tree of the Stuarts

James I

Charles I

Mary   Charles II   James II

William III   m.   Mary II   Queen Anne

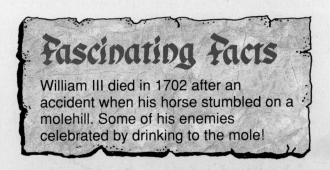

Fascinating Facts

William III died in 1702 after an accident when his horse stumbled on a molehill. Some of his enemies celebrated by drinking to the mole!

◀ Charles I 1625-1649

Charles I, son of James I, was born in Scotland in 1603. He was a shy child with a stutter, and grew to only 1.5 metres tall.

Charles was very religious and supported the English Church, but he believed that God had made him king, so he did not need to consult Parliament or his people. This attitude led to a civil war between the Royalists, who supported the king, and the Roundheads, who supported Parliament. Charles was defeated, and the Civil War ended with his execution.

▶ Charles II 1660-1685

After the death of his father, Charles I, Charles II invaded England with an army of Scots who had crowned him king. He was defeated and escaped to France, where he lived in poverty for nine years. Charles was invited back to England in 1660 as King Charles II. He was determined not to lose his throne again.

Charles II was a skilful, fun-loving ruler, and was given the nick-name of the 'merry monarch'. He had no children, so on his death in 1685, his brother James II succeeded him.

◀ James II 1685-1688

James II was an unpopular monarch because he tried to rule without Parliament. He was a Catholic, and gave Catholics important positions in the government and the army. He reigned for only three years before he was deposed and replaced by his daughter Mary, and her Protestant husband William of Orange. James fled to France, where he died in 1701.

William III and Mary II 1689-1702 ▶

When Mary was offered the throne of England, she insisted that her Dutch husband be crowned along with her. Afterwards, Mary left much of the business of the kingdom to William. Known as William of Orange, William was never popular. His English was poor, he had bad table manners and he seemed to be more interested in Holland than in England. William and Mary had no children, so the crown passed to Mary's sister Anne.

◀ Queen Anne 1702-1714

Anne, the last of the Stuart monarchs, was the second daughter of James II, and a firm supporter of the Church of England. In 1707 the Act of Union joined England and Scotland together, and Anne was the first monarch to rule over the United Kingdom.

Anne had seventeen children, all of whom died before her. On her death in 1714 the throne passed to the House of Hanover.

ANGLICANS AND PURITANS

During Stuart times, religion was an important part of everyday life.

People believed very strongly in God and his influence on their lives. They thought that poor harvests, disease, storms and floods were signs of God's displeasure. Religion and religious conflict caused many of the events that took place in the seventeenth century.

When James I came to power, the Church of England was the official religion in England. As a supporter of the Church of England, James was welcomed by many people. The Puritans hoped that James would get rid of the remaining forms of Catholic worship in the Anglican Church. Catholics resented the new laws which James passed, forcing them to attend Anglican Church services on Sundays.

As an Anglican, James believed that people should be able to read the Bible for themselves, and he ordered a new English translation. It was called the Authorised Version and could be found in every church in England. Produced by 54 scholars, it was first published in 1611 and is still used all over the world today.

▲ *The title page of the Authorised Version of the Bible, published in 1611.*

During the Stuart period conflict between Catholics and Protestants was not the only religious division. Some Protestants saw the Anglican Church as little better than the Catholic Church and challenged its authority. These people called themselves Puritans because they wanted to 'purify' the Church.

◄ *During the years that the Commonwealth ruled Britain (1649-1660) Puritan soldiers destroyed religious things, such as statues. This 15th century window in a Norfolk church only survived because it was taken out and hidden.*

The Roman Catholic Church The Pope, based in the Vatican City in Rome, Italy, is the head of the Catholic Church. Roman Catholics believe that the Pope is God's representative on earth. Bishops and priests help people understand and obey the ministry or teachings of the church.

Puritans Puritans believed that Christians should find out about Christian teachings by reading the Bible for themselves. They wanted to get rid of the bishops and to have a much simpler church service.

Anglicans Anglicans worship in the Church of England. The monarch is the Head of the Church, and the ministry of the church is organised by bishops, priests and deacons.

Fascinating Facts

During times of religious conflict, many rich Catholics hid priests in their houses. Some country mansions had a 'priest-hole' built into the walls where the priest could hide.

◀ *Archbishop Laud ordered many Puritans' ears to be cut off for criticising the government's religious policy. This cartoon shows him dining off the ears of a well-known Puritan, William Prynne.*

▼ *Scottish Puritans rioted against the authority of the bishops and the Anglican prayer book during the Prayer Book riot in St Giles Cathedral, Edinburgh in 1637.*

GUNPOWDER, TREASON AND PLOT

James I's mother was a Catholic, so when he came to the throne, the Catholics hoped for great changes.

However, they were very disappointed. James brought in new laws to banish Catholic priests. Catholics had to pay large fines if they were found hiding a priest in their home, or if they didn't attend Anglican church services on Sunday. In 1604, a group of Catholics, led by Robert Catesby and Thomas Percy, decided to blow up the king and the House of Lords at the state opening of Parliament.

The plotters asked Guy Fawkes, an explosives expert, to join them. Percy rented the building next door to Parliament, and Guy Fawkes pretended to be his servant. The plotters first tried to tunnel under the House of Lords, but the walls were too thick. Percy then rented a cellar underneath the House of Lords. He hid 36 barrels of gunpowder under piles of wood, where it lay hidden for seven months.

▲ Today the failure of the Gunpowder Plot is commemorated by the burning of a 'guy' and fireworks on November 5th.

▲ The Houses of Parliament as they are today.

▼ The lantern that Guy Fawkes used.

Fascinating Facts

Even today, Parliament's cellars and underground passages are regularly inspected. Although they are now lit by electricity, the officer always carries a lighted lantern.

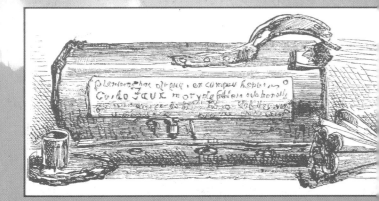

The plot was discovered when Frances Tresham, one of the plotters, wrote a letter warning his cousin, Lord Monteagle, to stay away from the opening of Parliament. Monteagle showed the letter to the king's chief minister, Robert Cecil. The cellars were searched at midnight on 4 November 1605 and Guy Fawkes was discovered guarding the gunpowder. He was arrested and tortured by order of the king. The other plotters tried to start an armed rebellion, but eight died and the rest were brought to London for trial with Guy Fawkes. They were all sentenced to death, and were hung, drawn and quartered in January 1606, opposite the building they had tried to blow up.

> ❛ My lord, out of the love I bear to some of your friends, I have a care of your preservation, and therefore I advise you as you tender your life to devise some excuse to shift your attendance at this parliament, for God and man hath concurred to punish the wickedness of this time. ❜
>
> **From the unsigned letter of 30 October 1605, warning Lord Monteagle to stay away from Parliament.**

▲ *The conspirators were hung on the gallows, then they were cut down and had their insides taken out, before their bodies were cut up, or quartered.*

▼ *The Gunpowder Plot conspirators. Here Guy Fawkes is called Guido Fawkes.*

Robert Winter   Christopher Wright   Iohn Wright   Thomas Percy   Guido Fawkes   Robert Catesby   Thomas Winter

KING AND PARLIAMENT

James I believed that he was chosen by God to be the king.

He expected everyone, including Parliament, to obey him without question.

This was called 'the divine right of kings'. James I was very extravagant, and Parliament deliberately kept him short of money in the hope that he would do what they wanted.

When James died in 1625, Parliament refused to give Charles I, his successor, any money to pay for the war against Spain. Charles tried to raise money by illegal taxes which people refused to pay. Eventually, Charles had to sign a document agreeing that nobody should be forced to pay a tax that had not been approved by Parliament. Charles, who also believed in the divine right of kings, decided to rule without Parliament. He tried many ways of raising money, including a special tax called 'ship money' to pay for the cost of building new ships for the navy. For two years, Charles quarrelled with Parliament, which tried to pass new laws to control him. On 4 January 1642, Charles went to the House of Commons to arrest the five leading members of Parliament who were against him, but they escaped before he arrived.

Charles was now so unpopular that there were riots in London. In 1642 civil war broke out between the Parliamentarians and the King and his supporters, who were called the Royalists.

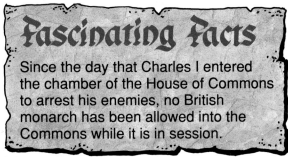

James I told Parliament in 1610 that:

❝ Kings are God's lieutenants upon earth and sit upon God's throne. ❞

◀ *Charles I spent a lot of money on works of art, like this ceiling, painted by Rubens: it shows James I swapping his earthly crown for a heavenly one.*

Fascinating Facts

Since the day that Charles I entered the chamber of the House of Commons to arrest his enemies, no British monarch has been allowed into the Commons while it is in session.

◀ *King James in Parliament, with Prince Charles (the future Charles I) on his left.*

▼ *Charles I enters the House of Commons to try and arrest his five leading opponents.*

CAVALIERS AND ROUNDHEADS

During the English Civil War, father fought against son and brother against brother.

Most of the big towns, including London and the south-east, supported Parliament. Wales, the north and west of the country, and half of the nobles, were in favour of the king. However, the clearest division between the two sides was a religious one. Puritans were more likely to be on the side of Parliament, while most Catholics were Royalists.

The king's army won the first battle of the war at Edgehill, near Birmingham. The Roundheads, led by Oliver Cromwell, defeated the Royalists at the battle of Marston Moor, near York, in 1644.

In 1645 Parliament created the New Model Army, which was well-equipped with guns and new uniforms. It defeated the king's troops at the battle of Naseby in Leicestershire.

The fighting continued until 1646. The King then gave himself up to the Scots, who handed him over to the Parliamentarians for a payment of £40,000. Charles escaped to the Isle of Wight in 1648. There were small uprisings throughout the country in his support, but Cromwell quickly defeated these, and Charles was put in prison.

▶ A crowd watched the execution of Charles II on 30 January 1649. The King removed his jacket and lay down with his head on a wooden block. He was then beheaded.

It was clear to Cromwell that while the king was alive there would always be conflict. He decided to put Charles on trial for treason. Charles was sentenced to death in London as a 'Tyrant, Traitor, Murderer and a public enemy'. On 30 January 1649, Charles was taken to Whitehall and beheaded. England was now a republic.

The Civil War had not quite ended, because the Scots proclaimed the king's son King Charles II. Cromwell defeated them at the battle of Dunbar in 1650, and Charles II was finally defeated at the battle of Worcester in 1651. Charles escaped and, after a series of adventures, crossed the Channel to France.

◀ When Charles was tried at Westminster, the President of the court wore a metal hat because he was afraid that the Royalists might try to kill him.

Fascinating Facts

Charles had many adventures after the battle of Worcester. He hid in an oak tree while Cromwell's men searched for him, and later escaped disguised as a servant before he finally sailed to France from Brighton.

◄ *Oliver Cromwell in 1649.*

WEAPONS AND WARFARE

Armies in the Stuart period had different kinds of soldiers: pikemen, musketeers, cavalry and dragoons.

▶ *This picture of the Battle of Naseby, fought in 1645, shows some of the different sorts of soliders who fought in the Civil War.*

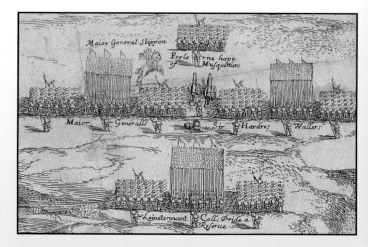

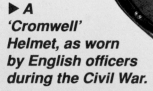

▶ *A 'Cromwell' Helmet, as worn by English officers during the Civil War.*

Pikemen *carried long wooden spears called pikes. They wore helmets on their heads, and armour on their chests, backs and thighs.*

Musketeers *wore very little armour. They carried long, heavy guns called muskets, and wore bandoliers or belts across their shoulders, with twists of paper full of gunpowder tied to them.*

The cavalry *was the most important part of an army. They were mounted on horseback, and wore armour. They carried swords and a pair of pistols which could fire one shot each.*

Dragoons *were soldiers on horseback who were armed with guns called carbines.*

At the beginning of a battle, pikemen stood in squares in the centre of each army. Musketeers fought in three rows, one row kneeling, one stooping and one standing. The first row of musketeers would fire a round while the other rows loaded their guns. The enemy's cavalry would charge down on the squares of pikemen and fire their pistols at them, then draw their swords and try to break up the squares. The horses often got impaled on the pikes. The battle continued with bloody hand-to-hand fighting until one side or the other gave up, or night forced them to stop.

▼ **These men, dressed in the uniform of the New Model Army, re-enact battles fought during the English Civil War.**

▲ *A pikeman.*

LIFE UNDER THE PURITANS

Now there was no king, a Council of State was set up to rule the country, or Commonwealth as it was called.

In 1653, Oliver Cromwell decided to rule the country without Parliament. He was supported by the army.

Cromwell was a Puritan, and he passed laws to make everyone else live as Puritans. Everybody had to go to church on Sundays, holy days were abolished and clothing and food had to be plain and simple. Churches were stripped of all their statues, stained glass windows and decorated altars. Nobody was allowed to work on a Sunday, and even cooking or going for a walk was forbidden. People who broke these rules were fined or put in the stocks. One man was fined ten shillings for walking to the next village to hear a sermon on a Sunday, and a girl was put in the stocks for mending her dress on the Sabbath.

▲ *Puritans did not like religious symbols. In 1643 they pulled down the cross in Cheapside, London.*

▼ *Cromwell dissolves Parliament in 1653. On the wall is written 'This house is to let'.*

THIS HOVSE IS TO LETT

The father was the head of the Puritan family and would lead prayers in the home two or three times a day. Children were expected to learn large passages of the Bible by heart. They had to obey adults at all times.

Puritans worked hard. They thought it was sinful to waste time enjoying themselves, so they banned theatres, football, dancing round the maypole and other popular pastimes. Celebrating Christmas and Easter was also forbidden. Instead they were turned into fast days, when people were encouraged to go without food, pray and think about their sins.

Music was the only form of entertainment allowed, and many people enjoyed singing and playing musical instruments. Reading was encouraged and many religious pamphlets and sermons were published.

▲ Puritans wore simple clothes with plain white collars.

▲ A Puritan family reading aloud from the Bible.

Fascinating Facts

Children were expected to remember the sermons they heard in church. At the age of four, Lucy Hutchinson, a Puritan child, could read English perfectly and repeat sermons word for word.

▶ People who did not attend church services were put in the stocks.

ROYALTY RETURNS

Before Oliver Cromwell died in 1658, he named his son Richard as his successor.

However, Richard did not want to rule and he soon resigned. The Army generals quarrelled with Parliament and argued among themselves. In 1660 General Monck wrote to Charles, son of King Charles I, in Holland, inviting him to become King Charles II. This return of a king to the English throne is known as the 'Restoration'.

Many people were pleased when Charles rode into London in 1660. The new king had learned many French fashions during his exile in France, and his court was lively and civilised. Ordinary people once again enjoyed pleasures such as going to the theatre, painting, music, dancing and gambling.

Within a year the power of the Puritans had collapsed. Nine of the fifty-nine people who had signed Charles I's death warrant were executed. New laws were passed to strengthen the position of Anglicans in place of the Catholics and Puritans.

People were still worried about the Catholics, and there were many rumours of plots.

▲ *A mug celebrating the coronation of Charles II.*

▶ *Charles II enters London, 1660.*

Titus Oates made up details of a 'Popish Plot' to murder Charles and kill the Protestants. His story was proved to be false, but many Catholics had already been blamed for the plot, and executed or imprisoned.

When Charles II died in 1685, his brother James II became king. James II was unpopular with many of his people because of his strong Catholic beliefs and his belief in the divine right of the king. In 1685, the Duke of Monmouth led a Protestant rebellion, which was quickly defeated. Monmouth was beheaded and his followers were severely punished. However, James's unpopularity increased when he allowed Catholics to take up official positions in the navy, army and local councils.

▲ *A painting of William and Mary.*

When James's son was born, Parliament was afraid that England would become a Catholic country once again. They wrote to Mary, the eldest daughter of James II, and her husband, William of Orange, inviting them to come to England and save the Protestant faith. When William landed in Devon in 1688 with an army of Dutchmen, James II, remembering the fate of his father Charles I, threw the Great Seal (the royal stamp needed for all official documents) into the River Thames and fled to France.

❝ *If I do not retire I shall certainly be sent to the Tower and no king ever went out of that place but to his grave. It is a cruel thing for a subject to be driven out of his native country, much more for a King to be driven out of his three Kingdoms.* ❞

From a speech by James II.

THE DEADLY PLAGUE

During the reign of Charles II, London was noisy, dirty, smelly and crowded.

Rubbish was thrown into the streets from houses, shops and warehouses. It was collected by men called scavengers who either threw it into the river, or left it in huge rotting piles outside the city walls. Rats and other vermin bred in these piles, while fleas and lice lived in people's dirty clothes. These unhealthy conditions encouraged disease and death.

In May 1665, poor people living in the overcrowded houses of London began to die from the plague, or Black Death. Bad outbreaks of the plague, which was passed on to people by rats' fleas, had occurred many times in Britain over the previous 200 years, but this one proved to be the worst. By August many rich people, including the king and his court, had left London to escape the plague. Shops were shut and the streets were deserted.

Women, called 'searchers', were paid 2p a day to find out the cause of all deaths within the city. When a person died of the plague, a red cross was painted on the door and the family was nailed up inside the house for 40 days. No one except doctors or searchers was allowed to enter or leave. Whole families died shut up in their homes.

▶ *Doctors tried to protect themselves against infection by wearing long leather gowns with hoods and gloves. The beak of the mask was stuffed with herbs, and the eyes were made of glass.*

At night, handcarts were pulled through the streets to the sound of ringing bells and shouts of 'Bring out your dead'. Soon all the churchyards were full, and huge graves called plague-pits were dug to bury the bodies. In September the number of deaths was over 1,000 a day. With the colder weather of autumn and winter, the number of deaths grew less and the plague eventually disappeared. Over 60,000 Londoners had died.

Some of the people who fled from London carried the disease with them. The plague seems to have travelled to Eyam, a village in Derbyshire, in a box of clothes sent to the village tailor. It is thought that 260 of the 300 inhabitants died. After July it was almost impossible to leave London without a health certificate, to protect against people spreading the disease.

> ❛ Walked to the tower. But Lord! How empty the streets are, and melancholy. So many poor sick people in the streets full of sores ... They tell me that in Westminster there is never a physician and but one apothecary left, all being dead. ❜

From Samuel Pepys' Diary.

▲ London citizens fled by boat and barge, on foot, in carts and on horseback. The second picture shows guards trying to prevent people entering a town, even though one person holds out a certificate to show he is free from plague. Those left behind had to cope with burying the dead, who were flung from carts into huge pits.

Fascinating Facts

Plague figures for London, 1665

May	43 deaths
June	600 deaths
July	4117 deaths
August	16,229 deaths
September	26,219 deaths
October	18,373 deaths
November	3454 deaths

◀ Lists of those who had died of the plague and other diseases were published every week.

The Diseases and Casualties this Week.

Abortive	5	Imposthume	11
Aged	43	Infants	16
Ague	2	Killed by a fall from the Belfrey at Alhallows the Great	1
Apoplexie	1	Kingsevil	2
Bleeding	2	Lethargy	1
Burnt in his Bed by a Candle at St.Giles Cripplegate	1	Palsie	1
		Plague	7165
Canker	1	Rickets	17
Childbed	42	Rising of the Lights	11
Chrisomes	18	Scowring	5
Consumption	134	Scurvy	2
Convulsion	64	Spleen	1
Cough	2	Spotted Feaver	101
Dropsie	33	Stilborn	17
Feaver	309	Stone	2
Flox and Small-pox	5	Stopping of the stomach	9
Frighted	3	Strangury	1
Gowt	1	Suddenly	1
Grief	3	Surfeit	49
Griping in the Guts	51	Teeth	121
Jaundies	5	Thrush	5
		Timpany	1
		Tissick	11
		Vomiting	3
		Winde	3
		Wormes	15

Christned {	Males — 95	Buried {	Males — 4095
	Females — 81		Females — 4202
	In all — 176		In all — 8297

Plague — 7165

Increased in the Burials this Week — 607
Parishes clear of the Plague — 4   Parishes Infected — 126

The Assize of Bread set forth by Order of the Lord Maior and Court of Aldermen;
A penny Wheaten Loaf to contain Nine Ounces and a half, and three half-penny White Loaves the like weight.

LONDON'S BURNING

Between 2 and 6 September 1666, a great fire swept through London.

The summer of 1666 was long and hot. By autumn the wooden buildings were bone dry. During the early morning of 2 September 1666, fire broke out in the house of Thomas Farynor, a baker in Pudding Lane. Farynor and his family escaped through an upstairs window, but their maidservant refused to jump, and was burned to death. She was the first casualty of the fire.

A strong east wind blew sparks from the fire into the neighbouring Thames Street, where cellars and warehouses were filled with goods which quickly caught alight. Soon the whole area was ablaze and even buildings on London Bridge were on fire. The king ordered the Lord Mayor to pull down any houses in the path of the fire, but the fire kept overtaking them.

By the morning of Monday 3 September, the fire had reached the centre of the City, and the streets were jammed with people pushing barrows piled high with their belongings as they tried to escape. Boats carried people to safety across the river. King Charles and his brother James now took command of the fire-fighting. They stood up to their ankles in water helping the chains of men pass buckets of water from hand to hand.

The fire burnt itself out on the fifth day. Most of the older part of London had been destroyed, and thousands of people were made homeless.

Charles ordered that the city was to be rebuilt in brick and stone. Sir Christopher Wren drew up designs for a new city with wide streets and squares. This new city was never built, because people who had lost their houses wanted them built exactly where they had been before. But Wren built at least 60 new churches and a tall column called the Monument which marks the spot where the fire began. Wren's most famous building, St Paul's Cathedral, took 35 years to build.

Fascinating Facts

There was no fire brigade in those days. Chains of men passed leather buckets of water from hand to hand to try to put out the fire. Other people used small hand pumps, called squirts, and long hooks to pull the thatch off the houses.

◀ A leather bucket, and a squirt used during the fire.

❛ The churches, houses, and all on fire, and flaming at once, and a horrid noise the flames made, and the cracking of houses at their ruin. ❜

From the Diary of Samuel Pepys.

▶ We know a lot about day-to-day events in Stuart times, including the plague and the great fire of London, from the diaries of Samuel Pepys written between 1660 and 1669.

▲ Old Saint Paul's Cathedral burns during the Great Fire of London, while people crowd into boats to escape the fire.

MASSACRES AND REBELLIONS

During the Stuart period, English people thought of Ireland and Scotland as foreign countries.

Journeys to Scotland and Ireland were long and difficult. They had their own customs, culture and language, and Scotland had its own Parliament and laws. Although James I united the crowns of England and Scotland, the two countries were still separate in many ways.

During the reign of James I, English and Scottish Protestants were encouraged to settle in Ireland, where most people were Catholics. These settlers took the best farmland and treated the native Irish people very badly. In 1641 the Irish Catholics rebelled against the settlers. They attacked Protestant farms and murdered their owners. Over 2,000 Protestants were killed and thousands more were driven into hiding. When this news reached London, there were rumours that it was a Catholic plot to destroy Parliament.

Oliver Cromwell was determined to punish the Irish for the Protestant deaths in the rebellion. He landed in Ireland in 1649 with a large army, killed many people, and took away the lands of the Irish Catholics, which he gave to his Puritan soldiers. The Catholics were driven into the poorest lands in the west.

The Irish Catholics welcomed James II to the throne and supported him in his attempts to win back his crown. This made the Irish Protestants afraid of another massacre. William of Orange led an army to Ireland. He defeated James and his Catholic army at the Battle of the Boyne in 1690.

▼ *The Battle of the Boyne, 1690.*

▲ *This cartoon of 1649 shows Saint George, representing the soldiers of Cromwell, trampling on the Irish dragon.*

In Scotland religious differences between Catholics and Protestants were just as important. Towards the end of the century, most Highland chiefs were Catholics. They were called Jacobites because they supported James II. In 1689 there was a Jacobite uprising, but this was defeated.

The Highland chiefs were made to swear an oath of loyalty to King William by 1 January 1692. All the chiefs took the oath except for MacIan, chief of the Clan MacDonald, who was prevented by heavy snow from arriving in time. Sir John Dalrymple sent a troop of 120 men to Glencoe to punish MacIan. Among the troop were many Campbells, ancient enemies of the MacDonalds. They killed 38 members of the Clan MacDonald.

> 6 You are hereby ordered to fall upon the rebels, the MacDonalds of Glencoe and put all to the sword under 70. You are to have especial care that the old fox MacIan and his cubs do on no account escape your hands. You are to secure all avenues, that no man escape. This you are to put in execution at five in the morning precisely. 9

From the order issued by Major Robert Duncanson to Captain Campbell of Glenlyon.

▲ *Queen Anne signs the Act of Union, which joined England and Scotland in 1707.*

When Queen Anne came to the throne, Scotland and England were joined into one country with one Parliament. This Act of Union was very unpopular in Scotland and there were riots in Edinburgh. The people hoped that France would help them restore their rightful king. In 1708 the French King sent an expedition to Scotland under the command of James, James II's young son. But James fell ill with measles, and sailed away from Scotland without landing, losing the chance of winning back the throne.

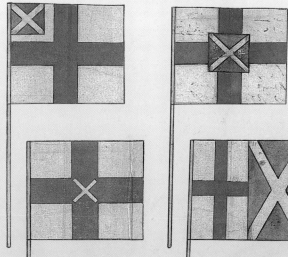

▲ *James I united the crowns of England and Scotland. These were some suggestions for how to unite the two flags.*

Fascinating Facts

Some Protestants in Northern Ireland still call themselves Orangemen after King William of Orange.

NEW LANDS AND COLONIES

During the 17th century many people from Europe went to live in the 'new' lands recently discovered in America.

Many of these people wanted the freedom to worship God in their own way. Others were merchants and traders who wanted to do business and get rich. Some people went to the colonies to escape from poverty. Others, such as the unemployed and the homeless, were kidnapped and sent to work in the colonies as hired labourers and servants. The original inhabitants of these areas were often treated badly and driven off their land by new settlers.

The first permanent English settlement in North America was made in Virginia at Jamestown, named after James I. Within a few years the settlers were growing and selling Virginian tobacco.

▶ *This is a model of the Mayflower which took the Pilgrim Fathers to found a new settlement in Massachusetts in 1620.*

In 1620 a group of Puritans, the Pilgrim Fathers, left Plymouth, England on a ship called the *Mayflower*. Some of them were hoping to make their fortunes, but most wanted to be free to worship God in the Puritan way. They landed on Cape Cod and started to build a settlement. During the first winter they suffered many hardships and half of them died. The next year, with the help of the local Indians, the Pilgrims learned to hunt and fish, and to plant crops. By 1630, nearly 1,000 Puritans had settled in this new colony in Massachusetts.

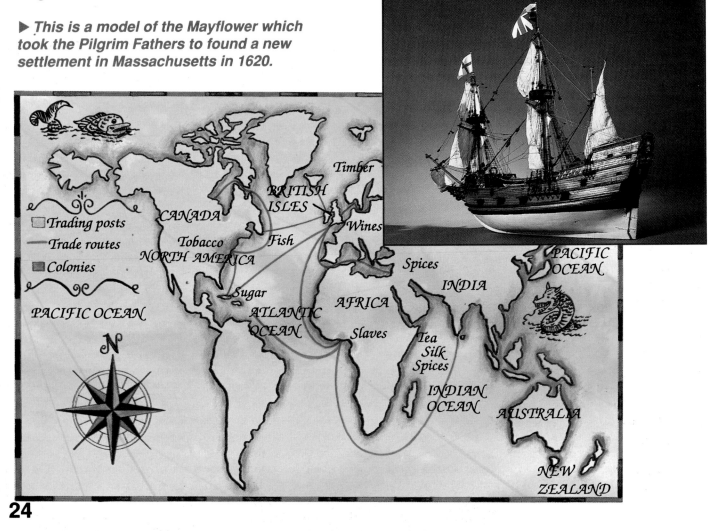

▲ *William Penn makes a treaty with the Native Americans in 1641 to buy land for a Quaker settlement.*

Fascinating Facts

The Royal African Company was given the right to trade in slaves along the west coast of Africa. The slaves were taken to the colonies in Virginia and the West Indies to work on the sugar plantations. By 1680, 5,000 slaves were arriving in Jamaica every year from Africa.

In 1634, Catholics established a colony at Maryland. Then in 1664 the English settlers drove out the Dutch settlers from New Amsterdam, and renamed it New York. In 1681, William Penn founded Pennsylvania as a settlement for strict Puritans called Quakers. Carolina, named after King Charles II, was founded in 1663. The English now had settlements all along the east coast of North America and on islands such as Jamaica and Bermuda in the West Indies. Jamaica supplied England with sugar, coffee, ginger and pepper.

Meanwhile English trading companies also carried goods to India, Africa and Russia. The East India Company set up trading stations in India and exchanged woollen cloth for Indian cotton goods, silks and spices.

▲ *Settlers build Jamestown, the first permanent English settlement in Virginia.*

NEWS AND VIEWS

During the Stuart period, interest in the printed word grew enormously.

When coffee was introduced into England early in the Stuart period, it became a very fashionable drink. Rich people met at coffee houses to talk business and discuss the latest news. They eagerly read the 'courants', or news books, that were published either weekly or monthly. The first English newspaper, the *Weekley Newes,* was published in 1622.

Writers and poets of the time took part in the arguments that led to the Civil War. Many people wrote articles in favour of or against the king. During the Civil War, the printing houses of Fleet Street in London kept up a continuous flow of news sheets, cartoons and pamphlets in support of one side or the other.

After the war, Cromwell banned many of the news sheets, and only Puritan writings were encouraged. When Charles II first returned to the throne, there was a flood of new newspapers, but the Licensing Act of 1662 allowed only two official newspapers to be published. Writers who wanted to criticise the government gave out pamphlets, often in coffee houses. In 1675 Charles tried to close the coffee houses because he felt they spread false gossip and rumours.

▼ *A cartoon showing Charles imprisoned in Carisbrook Castle on the Isle of Wight.*

Behold your King

THE ILE OF WAIT

Fascinating Facts

Edward Lloyd first issued *Lloyd's News* from his coffee house in 1688. *Lloyd's List* and *Lloyd's Shipping Index* are still published daily, and give details of over 21,000 ships and their daily movements all over the world.

◀ **People gathered in coffee houses to meet their friends and read the newspapers.**

◀ **Charles II's proclamation of 1675, which tried to close the coffee houses.**

By the King.

A PROCLAMATION
FOR THE
Suppression of Coffee-Houses.

CHARLES R.

God save the King.

After the Glorious Revolution, when Mary and William of Orange took over the throne, the freedom to publish newspapers increased. At this time the first local newspapers appeared, including the *Worcester Post* (1690) and the *Edinburgh Gazette* (1699). After 1691 the postal system improved so much that it became possible to publish the first daily newspaper, the *Daily Courant*. Many well-known writers such as Jonathan Swift, Daniel Defoe, Sir Richard Steele, and Joseph Addison now wrote for the newspapers. They commented on, and made fun of, the politicians of the day. Many people's ideas, then as now, were influenced by what they read in the papers.

27

SCIENCE AND SCHOLARSHIP

The Stuart period was an important time for new scientific discoveries and inventions.

Scholars wrote to each other and formed societies to discuss their interests. From 1645 a group of people interested in scientific discoveries began meeting regularly in Oxford and London. In 1662 Charles II gave them a charter that founded the Royal Society. Its members carried out weekly experiments and collected information about all sorts of different topics.

Charles II was very interested in science and astronomy. In 1675 he commissioned Christopher Wren to build the Royal Observatory, where scientists could study the stars in aid of navigation.

William Harvey (1578-1657) studied medicine and became court physician to King James I and King Charles I. Using birds and animals, he made a careful study of the heart and blood vessels and discovered how blood circulated round the body. His discovery changed the way doctors and surgeons worked, but at the time many people thought he was mad.

Isaac Newton (1642-1727), physicist and mathematician and one of the greatest scientists of all time, made three important discoveries.

He discovered the theory of gravity while sitting in an orchard. He saw an apple fall and decided that this must be because the earth attracted the apple. From this, he realised that, just as the force of gravity pulled the apple to the ground, gravity keeps the moon in its orbit around the earth.

Newton also discovered that white light is a mixture of seven different colours. He showed how to pass a beam of sunlight through a prism so that it splits into the seven colours of the spectrum – violet, indigo, blue, green, yellow, orange and red. As a result of his study of light he invented the mirror telescope. Newton also introduced the branch of mathematics called calculus.

▼ Harvey showed that blood only flows in one direction. By applying finger pressure to different veins he worked out which way the blood was flowing.

▶ Sir Isaac Newton is remembered above all for his ideas on gravity.

Edmund Halley (1656-1742) was a brilliant astronomer. He studied the motion of bodies around the sun. He was the first person to work out that a bright comet, now named Halley's comet, would return according to its orbit. Halley also made important studies of the earth's magnetism, tides and weather. He listed over 300 stars, including a new constellation Robur Carolinum in honour of Charles.

> *On the morning of the 25th his Highness . . . went in his carriage . . . to Arundel House, in the interior of Gresham College . . . for the sittings of the academy or Royal Society, which meets every Thursday after dinner to take cognizance of matters of natural philosophy, and the study and examination of chemical, mechanical and mathematical subjects.*

From Count Lorenzo Magalotti's description of the Royal Society, 1669.

◄ *Edmond Halley worked out the paths around the sun of 24 comets.*

► *Sir Isaac Newton's mirror telescope.*

▼ **The Royal Observatory at Greenwich.**

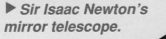

TRANSPORT AND TRAVEL

During Stuart times travel was dangerous and difficult.

Most people rarely left the town or village where they were born.

The roads were poor and deeply rutted. In winter, bad weather could sweep away bridges. Snowstorms and snowdrifts could block roads for weeks. Highwaymen lay in wait to rob travellers of their possessions.

Poor people usually walked from village to village. Others travelled on horseback. Inn-keepers kept post horses which could be hired out to travellers. Wealthy women often rode on a special side-saddle behind a servant.

Only the very rich had coaches, and these were uncomfortable. The windows had no glass and there were few springs. After the Restoration,   new lighter chariots were introduced.

In towns, people could hire hackney carriages and sedan chairs to take them through the narrow, crowded streets. A sedan chair was carried by two or four men.

From 1640, people who could afford it travelled by public stage wagons. These travelled in short stages at a cost of a shilling for every five miles. The wagon stopped at inns where the travellers could rest and the horses could be changed.

Heavy goods were often transported by water. Rivers were deepened so boats and barges could pass along them. Covered 'tilt' boats carried passengers. Other heavy goods went by clumsy horse-drawn wagons, which in winter often tipped over or got stuck in the mud. Many goods were carried in baskets by pack horses or donkeys. Travellers often joined these trains of animals to protect themselves from highwaymen.

▲ Sedan chairs were common in the 17th century.

From 1635 a regular post, available to everyone, was carried along the main roads from London. Each village had its own postmaster who sent postboys out to deliver the letters.

From 1663 tollgates were built on the main roads. Travellers had to pay a fee to use a stretch of road. The money was supposed to be used to repair the road, but this didn't always happen. The constant stopping at tollgates made journeys even slower.

Celia Fiennes (1622-1741) was a well-off Puritan woman, who travelled about 3000 miles on horseback through England. She wrote a journal which describes her travels and tells us a lot about the countryside in the later Stuart period.

She describes how near Wymondham:

❝ the road on the causey was in many places full of holes, though it is secured by a bar at which passengers pay a penny a horse in order to the mending of the way, for all about is not to be rode on unless it is a very dry summer. ❞

◀ *A string of loaded packhorses.*
▼ *A 17th century carriage.*

Fascinating Facts

Stage coach journeys from London to Salisbury took two days; London to Exeter took four days; London to York took four days. Today, all of these journeys can be completed in less than three hours.

◀ *These boots were worn to protect the legs of postilions, who rode the horses that pulled a coach.*

▼ *Stage wagons were ordinary carts covered by cloth. They carried goods and passengers together.*

INDEX